THE ACHIEVERS

SHAQUILLE O'NEAL
Center of Attention

Brad Townsend

Lerner Publications Company ■ Minneapolis

Information for this book was obtained from the following sources: *San Antonio Light, San Antonio Express News, Boston Globe, Orlando Sentinel, USA Today, New York Times Magazine, Philadelphia Inquirer, Florida Today Magazine, and Fort Worth Star-Telegram, Star Tribune, Forbes, Sports Illustrated.*

This book is available in two editions:
Library binding by Lerner Publications Company
Soft cover by First Avenue Editions
241 First Avenue North, Minneapolis, Minnesota 55401

International Standard Book Number: 0-8225-2879-7 (lib bdg.)
International Standard Book Number: 0-8225-9655-5 (pbk.)

LIBRARY OF CONGRESS CATALOGING-IN-PUBLICATION DATA

Townsend, Brad.
  Shaquille O'Neal, center of attention / by Brad Townsend.
    p. cm. — (The Achievers)
  ISBN 0-8225-2879-7 (lib. bdg.)
  ISBN 0-8225-9655-5 (pbk.)
  1. O'Neal, Shaquille—Juvenile literature. 2. Basketball players—United States—Biography—Juvenile literature. [1. O'Neal, Shaquille. 2. Basketball players. 3. Afro-Americans—Biography.] I. Title. II. Series.
GV884.054T69 1994
796.323'092—dc20   93-35558
[B]

Page 2: Movie strongman Arnold Schwarzenegger (left) looks up to basketball's big man, Shaquille O'Neal.

Contents

Fun-Loving Giant

In many ways, he is still a kid. He loves pizza, orange soda pop, martial arts movies, and rap music. Sometimes he plays his music so loud the walls of his house shake and the neighbors complain. He owns so many video games that his house resembles an arcade. And sometimes, after basketball practice, he entertains his teammates by rapping or break dancing, spinning his 7-foot, 1-inch, 305-pound body on the floor like a huge top.

Shaquille O'Neal is a powerful force on the basketball court, but he was just 20 when he entered the National Basketball Association (NBA) and instantly became a star. In the span of a few months, he signed a 7-year, $40 million contract to play for Orlando, bought a $700,000 mansion next to a golf course, and became the first rookie to start in an NBA All-Star game since Michael Jordan in 1985.

Although he entered the NBA at an age when most players still are sophomores or juniors in college, Shaquille has quickly established himself as one of the game's premier centers, alongside Hakeem Olajuwon, Patrick Ewing, and David Robinson.

On July 1, 1996, Shaquille became a free agent. That meant that he could play for any team. Although practically every team in the NBA wanted him, he decided to join the L.A. Lakers. He signed a seven-year contract with them for about $120 million.

Certainly, Shaquille's best basketball years are yet to come. "The scary thing is that Shaq's not only bigger than everybody else, but he's getting smarter all the time," said NBA center Sean Rooks. "Every time we took something away from him, he just found another way to beat us."

While he continues to learn and improve on the court, Shaquille is still playful. "I like toys, and I like my music," he said. "If I wasn't a basketball player, I'd be a rapper or a comedian." No doubt his move to Los Angeles brings him closer to the center of music and entertainment.

Shaquille likes his cars, too. The license plate on his maroon Ford Explorer reads "SHAQ ATAK." The license plate on his black Mercedes reads "SHAQNIFICENT."

Shaquille likes to relax by driving in his Ford Explorer with the Shaq Atak license plates.

He bought a Mercedes for his parents and a Mustang for one of his sisters. And when he drives, he usually has the windows down, a big smile on his face, and the music blaring as loud as possible.

His smile, as much as his basketball ability, has helped make Shaquille an instant fan favorite. His picture has been on the cover of every major sports

9

magazine. And his TV commercials for Pepsi-Cola and Reebok have helped make him a worldwide celebrity.

How rich has Shaquille become? He has made millions of dollars in product endorsement contracts with companies such as Pepsi, Reebok, Spalding sporting goods, and Kenner Parker Toys. In addition, he's planning to open a theme park in Orlando called "Shaq's Place." He will even have a line of "Shaq Snaqs," which includes a chocolate bar called "Mr. Big."

Never mind his age, and the fact that he promises to get even better—Shaquille is already among the league's stars. In his Rookie of the Year season in 1992–93, he finished second in the NBA in blocked shots per game (3.53), second in rebounds per game (13.9), and fourth in field goal percentage (.562). And he tied David Robinson for eighth in the NBA in scoring, 23.4 points per game.

"He's got it all," former Lakers star Magic Johnson said of Shaquille. "He's got the smile, and the talent and the charisma. And he's sure got the money, too."

Fame and money, however, are not as important to Shaquille as the kind of example he sets for his young fans. Above all, Shaquille wants to make the most of the gifts with which he has been blessed—on and off the court.

10

Shaquille finds a young fan in the hospital.

The intimidator who wears size-21 basketball shoes, and who twice during his rookie season pulled down the backboard after a dunk, also has a softer side. He cares deeply about people who are less fortunate than he.

On Thanksgiving 1992, Shaquille took time out from his rookie season to feed 300 homeless people at a shelter in Orlando. He dished out peas and rice, and to the homeless people's surprise, he sat down and ate with them. He spent two hours at the shelter, laid down a $7,000 check to cover all 300 meals, and called it "the best Thanksgiving ever."

"Basketball is not everything in life," he said. "Doesn't make a difference if they know me. As long as they can eat and they're happy."

11

At Christmas, Shaquille bought three truckloads of toys for underprivileged children. The Salvation Army and the Center for Drug-Free Living had provided Shaquille with a list of 120 children affected by drug abuse in their families. With a list of only the children's first names and ages, Shaquille made three trips to toy stores, picked the presents himself, brought them home, and had them wrapped in his living room. Then he personally delivered the presents.

Shaquille also often visits the Arnold Palmer Hospital for Women and Children near Orlando. "Nobody has to tell me to go visit a sick baby or help feed the homeless," Shaquille said. "I want to be big enough to do that for myself. It's something I'll keep on doing."

One reason Shaquille reaches out to young people is that not so long ago, he was a troubled teenager himself. He knows as well as anyone that young people need guidance. Before he became a basketball star, Shaquille admits he was a kid headed in the wrong direction, always looking for trouble.

"Thank goodness," he said, "I had two parents who loved me enough to stay on my case."

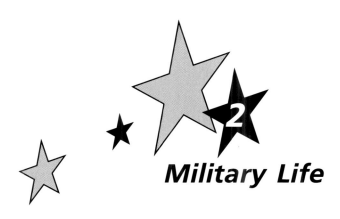

Military Life

One of the hardest things about Shaquille's child-hood, he admits, was having to move from place to place. Before Shaquille's parents, Philip Harrison and Lucille O'Neal, were married, they lived in Newark, New Jersey, struggling to make enough money to get by. In the early 1970s, Harrison decided to join the army. Before the couple could get married, the army sent Harrison to Germany. Lucille O'Neal was already pregnant with Shaquille, so Harrison was on an army base in Germany when Shaquille was born.

When the baby was born on March 6, 1972, Lucille decided to call him Shaquille Rashaun O'Neal. She saw the name Shaquille in a book of Islamic names and picked it because it means "Little Warrior." Philip Harrison soon returned from overseas and married Lucille. But they decided Shaquille would keep his mother's maiden name,

O'Neal. There were no men or boys on Lucille's side of the family, so Shaquille would keep alive the O'Neal name for future generations.

It didn't take long for young Shaquille to learn the life of a military child. Every three years, the army sent his father and his family to a new base. By the time Shaquille was 13, he had lived on army bases in New Jersey, Georgia, and the former West Germany.

By then Shaquille's family had grown to six. Lateefah was born six years after Shaquille, followed a year later by another sister, Ayesha, and by brother Jamal a year after that. Having a brother and sisters was nice, but it didn't change the fact that Shaquille had to make new friends every time the family moved.

Making matters even worse for Shaquille, he was growing at a rapid rate. By the time he was 13, he was 6 feet, 5 inches tall and had size-17 feet. Every time he started at a new army base school, the kids saw how big he was and figured he had flunked a few grades. Truth was, he was a year younger than most students in his grade because he started first grade when he was 5.

"I always got teased," Shaquille remembers. "Teased about my name. Teased about my size. Teased about being flunked.... It took a while to gain friends because people thought I was mean."

Philip and Lucille Harrison stand behind their children (left to right): Lateefah, Ayesha, Jamal, and Shaquille.

Shaquille was so self-conscious and ashamed of his height, he used to slouch. It was his way of trying to make himself look smaller. "My parents told me to be proud," he said, "but I wasn't. I wanted to be normal."

He just wanted to fit in with a group. As a result, he started making the wrong kind of friends. He ran around with a bad crowd, trying to act tough. Shaquille admits that when he lived in West Germany, he used to break into cars, stealing cassette tapes and other items. In school he used to start fights with kids and talk back to his teachers.

Shaquille hated living in West Germany. He thought that if he misbehaved, his parents might send him back to the United States to live with his grandmother. But his father had other ideas.

15

As an army sergeant, Harrison knew how to discipline men. He wanted Shaquille to understand the value of discipline, too. Even though Shaquille was as big as most men, his father was not exactly small at 6-foot-5. So Harrison never hesitated to paddle Shaquille when the boy got out of line.

One day at an army school gym in West Germany, 11-year-old Shaquille decided it would be fun to set off the fire alarm. Someone in his class told on him. The military police caught Shaquille and phoned his father. Harrison showed up at the military police station with a Ping-Pong paddle in his hand. He turned Shaquille over and spanked him in front of the military policemen.

In junior high school on the base in Fulda, West Germany, Shaquille liked to break-dance on the shop class floor. Wood shavings on the floor made it slippery and helped him spin, although the teacher kept telling him not to do it. One day Shaquille went with his parents to parent-teacher conferences. Before they went into the shop class to talk to the teacher, Harrison asked Shaquille if there was anything he and his mother should know.

"Oh, no," Shaquille answered. "Everything's fine." When they walked into the shop class, the teacher told Harrison that Shaquille was getting terrible grades. The teacher also told Harrison about Shaquille's break dancing on the shop floor.

Shaquille struggled at Fulda American School in Germany.

He told Harrison the first time he had caught Shaquille break dancing, he thought Shaquille "was having a seizure, or something."

Harrison stood up, grabbed Shaquille by the arm, took him to the nearest bathroom and spanked him. "Not because the teacher told me he was doing all that bad stuff," Harrison said. "But because I asked Shaquille if there was anything we needed to know, and he said everything was fine."

At home, Harrison established some of the same rules the men in his army unit had to follow. Harrison not only believed it was important for Shaquille to behave properly, he demanded that he dress neatly and be well groomed. One morning Shaquille came downstairs for breakfast neatly dressed and well behaved. His parents, however, suspected Shaquille was up to something. As Shaquille left for school, they told him, "Don't be surprised when you see us next."

Shaquille began playing basketball seriously when he was 13 and his family lived on an army base in West Germany.

Sure enough, soon after arriving at school, Shaquille forgot about the warning. He unbuttoned his shirt, rolled up his sleeves, and started running around the classroom, creating trouble. Suddenly, the classroom went quiet. Shaquille looked up and was shocked to see his father standing in the doorway. He lowered his head and slowly walked toward his father, knowing he had another spanking coming.

"I wasn't there to spy on him," Harrison said

later. "But sometimes when children get away from you, they tend to act differently. I wanted him to know that Daddy might not be there. Or he just might."

Soon, the discipline began to sink in. Shaquille got the message. When he was 13, he began to get serious about school and basketball. Really, his parents left him no choice. "I got spanked every day for a solid year," Shaquille remembered. "I mean every day. But I was a bad kid. I had it coming. At the time, I didn't see it. I didn't think they loved me. So one day, when all the other kids were out causing trouble, I picked up a basketball. I found a way out for myself."

The older Shaquille got, the more he understood that his parents punished him for a reason. They loved him. They wanted him to become the best person he could be. They wanted him to care about and have respect for everyone around him. Harrison says he hated the idea of hitting Shaquille, but that he felt his son should learn discipline at home. When Harrison was a child, his parents also believed in the importance of discipline at home.

"When we were coming up, our parents spanked us," Harrison said. "Not to a point where we were black and blue, but to teach us a right way and a wrong way. I'd rather do it [punish his children] than have somebody in the street do it."

19

As a child, Shaquille had dreamed of being a dancer, a break dancer, like those he used to watch on the TV show *Fame*. The larger he grew, however, the less graceful he became. The basketball court was the one place where his size was an advantage, a place where he could gain other kids' respect and feel good about himself. As he improved and began to be a dominant basketball player, kids stopped teasing him. He stopped hanging around with the wrong crowd. His grades improved, too.

About that time, in West Germany, Shaquille met the man who would later become his college basketball coach. Louisiana State University coach Dale Brown was conducting basketball clinics at army bases in West Germany. One day after a clinic near Fulda, he was so impressed with 6-foot-5 Shaquille's play that he walked up and asked him: "How long have you been in the army, soldier?" Answered Shaquille: "I'm not in the army, sir. I'm only 13."

Brown left the gym that day in shock. But he was wise enough to ask Shaquille to think about playing at LSU—when he was old enough, that is.

Stardom in San Antonio

It was February 1987 when Joel Smith, athletic director at Cole High School in San Antonio, received a phone call he would never forget. The caller was the school principal, telling Smith that Cole High had a new student.

New arrivals were nothing special for Smith. Cole's campus is on an army base, Fort Sam Houston, and 98 percent of its 300 students are sons or daughters of service members. Since many military families move every two or three years, students come and go at Cole all the time. But as Smith was about to find out, this new student was unique.

"You'd better get up here real quick," the excited principal told Smith. "We've got a big one coming in."

"Big" was right. When Smith got to the principal's office, there stood 6-foot-8 Shaquille O'Neal. He was 14 years old, a high school sophomore. His father, Philip Harrison, had been reassigned from the base in Fulda, West Germany, to San Antonio. Cole, one of the smallest high schools in San Antonio, had just accepted a kid who would soon become the most dominant basketball player in Texas high school history.

Shaquille had played two years of high school basketball in West Germany, mostly against other American army base schools. He had never scored fewer than 17 points in a game in West Germany. Since Shaquille transferred to Cole late in his sophomore year, his first game for the Cougars wouldn't be until his junior year.

"I had a lot of kids come in and say they were All-European or All-Germany or All-Whatever," Cole basketball coach Dave Madura said. "A lot of them had good stories; not a lot could produce. He [Shaquille] came in and I knew he'd play. I had seen films of him, but I really had no idea what he could do until about four games into his first season."

It didn't take long for Shaquille and the Cougars to capture the attention of San Antonio high school basketball fans. Under coach Madura, Cole already had a strong program, finishing 21-5 the year before Shaquille's arrival. But with Shaquille, the Cougars became almost unstoppable.

Ten games into Shaquille's first season, Cole was unbeaten and ranked second in Texas' Class 2A. Texas divides its schools into five classifications, according to the number of students enrolled in a school. The smallest schools are in Class A and the largest are in Class 5A. Most of the schools Cole played against didn't have many students, and few were outstanding athletes. Shaquille rarely faced an opponent who was taller than 6-foot-5.

Shaquille averaged 17.9 points, 13.3 rebounds, and 10 blocked shots per game during his junior season. Cole won its first 32 games and was just one victory away from advancing to the state semifinals. But then came a disappointment Shaquille would never forget. In the March 5, 1988, quarterfinal game against Liberty Hill, Shaquille was charged with three fouls in the first two minutes. He spent most of the game on the bench, and Liberty Hill pulled off a 79-74 upset.

That loss, however, did not hurt Shaquille's appeal to college scouts. During the summer after his junior year, Shaquille grew to 6-foot-11. He also showed he could compete with the best young players in the nation, playing on San Antonio's Basketball Congress International team, which won the national title.

High school basketball brought Shaquille many honors.

That summer, Shaquille received more than 500 letters from colleges offering basketball scholarships. He was the most sought-after high school recruit in the country. He was being recruited so intensely that he decided to choose a college right away, so he could enjoy his senior season at Cole without pressure from college scouts. He finally narrowed his list to Louisville, North Carolina, North Carolina State, Illinois, and Louisiana State University—the team coached by the man he had met two years ago in West Germany, Dale Brown.

Shaquille picked LSU, explaining: "I gave everybody a fair shot. I just got along with the staff and the players better at LSU. I liked the philosophy there." Having Shaquille agree to play at LSU was a dream come true for coach Brown, who had fantasized about having Shaquille at LSU since that day on the army base in West Germany. After seeing Shaquille on that day, Brown had written letters to Shaquille and followed his high school career.

"When I first met him in Germany, I couldn't believe his size," Brown remembered. "Then his father walks up. I told him, 'Sergeant, I don't know if your son plays basketball or not, but I'd like to watch him grow. I can't believe his size.' His father told me, 'Coach Brown, I don't mean to be rude, but we couldn't care less about basketball. He is going to become an educated young man who can contribute to society. If basketball fits in, that's fine.' I said, 'Sir, you and I are going to become great friends.' I loved his bluntness and his attitude."

Even as Shaquille became more famous as a basketball player, his father made certain he remained disciplined on and off the basketball court. Once, during Shaquille's junior season, Harrison interrupted a game by walking onto the court and telling Shaquille to tuck in his jersey. Discipline, Harrison believed, was the best way to make certain his children would become productive adults.

"I've always told Shaquille that the world has too many followers," Harrison said. "What he needed to be was a leader."

Clearly, Shaquille was maturing. He maintained a B average in high school. And the more he showed he could handle responsibility, the more responsibility his father gave him. By the time he was a high school senior, Shaquille had no curfew; he could come and go as he pleased.

There were many reasons for Shaquille to smile for his Cole High School yearbook picture.

"He was showing me he could handle the situation," Harrison said. "I always told him that if you respect your elders and yourself, the situation will fall into place."

From time to time, Shaquille still showed his boyish, prankish side. Once, upon seeing the Cole principal in the gym during a practice, Shaquille grabbed him and held him upside down by his ankles, shaking him until all the change from his pockets had fallen to the floor. Everyone, including the principal, roared with laughter.

By then, many people at Cole knew and loved Shaquille. Unlike during his troublemaking days in West Germany, Shaquille fit in at Cole.

"There was no doubt he was going to be a big-time player, but he never flaunted it," his coach, Dave Madura, said. "He probably was the most popular kid in school. Because of the way he was, there wasn't any jealousy."

Since Shaquille entered his high school senior season with a scholarship to LSU already arranged, there was just one goal on his mind: a state championship. Shaquille had spent much of the summer lifting weights and had grown to 240 pounds, about 25 pounds more than his weight as a junior.

Since Cole High School had grown to slightly more than 300 students, the Cougars were assigned to the larger Class 3A for the 1988–89 season.

Most of the other high school basketball players in Texas couldn't play at Shaquille's level.

Liberty Hill, the only team to beat Cole during Shaquille's junior season, also was moved to Class 3A. The Cougars entered the season longing for a chance to avenge that loss.

Coach Madura knew the bigger and stronger Shaquille would be even more dominant on the court. But no one realized how dominant.

Shaquille averaged 29.9 points, 21.4 rebounds, and 10 blocks, and he shot 71 percent from the field (361 of 509), as Cole powered to another unbeaten regular season. In one game, he pulled down 41 rebounds, a San Antonio high school record.

As it turned out, Shaquille and the Cougars were just getting warmed up. In the play-offs, Shaquille scored 47 points against Lampasas, 41 against Hitchcock, and 35 against Corpus Christi West Oso. That left the Cougars in a familiar position—in the regional final against Liberty Hill.

"Last year I feel the refs robbed us," Shaquille said before the game. "They robbed us big time. I'm ready for them this time."

That was obvious from the game's early moments. Shaquille thundered his way to 44 points and pulled down 17 rebounds, as Cole won, 85-72, to advance to the Class 3A state semifinals. Said Liberty Hill coach Danny Henderson of Shaquille and the Cougars: "I've been going to state tournaments since 1970 and that's the best 3A team I've ever seen."

Cole continued its unstoppable roll at the state tournament in Austin. The Cougars defeated Hearne, 69-56, in the semifinals, behind Shaquille's 38 points and 20 rebounds. The next day, before 13,042 fans, Cole outbattled Clarksville, 66-60, for the Class 3A championship.

Shaquille had 19 points, 26 rebounds, and 6 assists in the high school title game. The date was March 11, 1989—five days after Shaquille's 17th birthday.

"I really wanted a car, but a state championship is a good present," Shaquille said. "I just wanted to win for the school, not myself. I didn't let the pressure get to me. None of us did."

That victory capped a memorable ride for Cole. The Cougars amassed a 68–1 record during Shaquille's two seasons. And Shaquille, who averaged 37 points and 22 rebounds during play-offs as a senior, finished his high school career by being named to McDonald's High School All America team—along with other future pro basketball players Kenny Anderson, Bobby Hurley, and Jimmy Jackson.

For coach Madura and most of the Cole players, the state championship was the sports accomplishment of a lifetime, something that would never be topped. But everyone knew it was only the beginning for Shaquille. At 17 years old, his potential was unlimited.

Even then, Shaquille was dreaming of playing professional basketball. "It looks easy," he said. "But I know it's not. It's a lot of work. I don't have the skills right now. I'll have to develop them. But it [an NBA career] is what I want."

Shaquille finished his high school career by helping Cole win the Texas state basketball championship.

Moments after the state championship victory, Shaquille was asked whether he wanted a nickname, something like Hakeem "The Dream" Olajuwon's, as he prepared to begin his college career at LSU. "Yeah," Shaquille responded, "Shaquille the Deal."

The LSU Years

On the day Shaquille O'Neal arrived on the LSU campus in Baton Rouge, Louisiana, black clouds filled the sky and a tornado blew through town. In a way, that day would set the tone for Shaquille's sensational, but sometimes stormy, three-year college career.

As the most highly regarded college freshman in the United States, Shaquille's life was about to change dramatically. Suddenly he was a nationally known figure. Fans would fill college arenas to cheer him, boo him, or just see him. And almost everything he did and everywhere he went would be reported in newspapers and magazines, and talked about on television and radio.

Shaquille was ready for the challenge, physically and mentally. During the summer before he entered LSU, he grew from 6-foot-11 to 7-foot-1. And by spending much of the summer carrying bricks at a construction job, he grew from 240 pounds to a powerful 290 pounds. Though he was 17, a year younger than most college freshmen, Shaquille was an intimidating sight for LSU opponents.

Off the court, Shaquille was mature enough to start college life, and to live away from home for the first time. His parents had taught Shaquille about respecting others, and about the importance of making his own decisions and living by them. When Shaquille decided to attend LSU, some people believed that Philip Harrison had made the choice for him. Actually, Harrison wanted Shaquille to attend North Carolina, but he had kept his opinion to himself. When Shaquille chose LSU, his parents supported him.

"That decision was his alone," Harrison said. "We pushed the boat away the day he decided to go there. We told him, 'Go out there and take what we taught you and what you learned in life and apply it and do what you have to do.'"

As if expectations weren't immense enough for Shaquille, he began his freshman season with LSU ranked second in the country by Associated Press sportswriters around the nation.

Shaquille dribbles downcourt for Louisiana State.

With high-scoring sophomore guard Chris Jackson and sophomore 7-footer Stanley Roberts back from a 20-12 season, the Tigers had plenty of returning talent—plus the player everyone couldn't wait to see: Shaquille O'Neal.

But right away, Shaquille discovered that playing major college basketball would be a learning experience. In his first game for the Tigers, Shaquille was whistled for three fouls during the first seven minutes. He finished the game with only 10 points.

It would be that kind of season for Shaquille and LSU—good, but not up to expectations. By the season's end, the Tigers had fallen to number 19 in the country, with Shaquille averaging 13.9 points and 12.0 rebounds. Their season ended in disappointment, with a 94-91 loss to Georgia Tech in the second round of the NCAA Tournament, despite 21 points by Roberts and 19 by Shaquille.

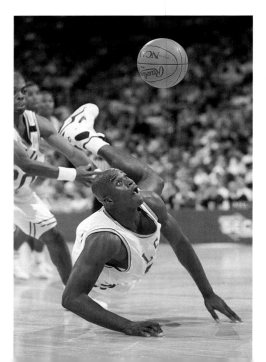

Shaquille's hustling, diving style excited fans of Louisiana State University's basketball team.

LSU coach Dale Brown (left) knew he wanted Shaquille in his huddle ever since he met him in Germany.

After the Georgia Tech loss, Jackson and Roberts announced they were leaving LSU before they graduated to play in the NBA. Immediately, that made Shaquille LSU's star, a player the Tigers would count on to score more.

He responded in a big way, averaging 27.6 points and 14.7 rebounds, making the cover of *Sports Illustrated,* and being named college basketball player of the year.

LSU's opponents often concentrated on guarding Shaquille.

But once again, the season ended in disappointment. Two weeks before the NCAA Tournament, Shaquille suffered a small fracture in his left leg.

The injury caused him to miss the Southeastern Conference Tournament. When Shaquille did return for the first round of the NCAA Tournament against Connecticut, he admitted he was rusty. Although he finished with 27 points, Connecticut knocked LSU out of the tournament, 79-62.

That ended the Tigers' season at 20-10, the second straight year they were beaten early in the tournament. But LSU had depended too much on Shaquille all season. Opposing teams often surrounded him, and his teammates were too inexperienced to take advantage of their opponents' concentration on Shaquille.

After the Connecticut loss, talk spread that Shaquille would leave LSU before graduating and become a professional player, as Jackson and Roberts had done the year before. Although he had just turned 19, basketball experts estimated Shaquille could make as much as $50 million by skipping his last two years at LSU and entering the NBA.

But there was one factor the experts didn't consider. Shaquille's parents had always wanted Shaquille to become the first one in their extended family to get a college degree. Shaquille had always dreamed of getting a degree, too. He surprised many fans by deciding to return to LSU for his junior year.

"People say, 'You could have 50 million,'" his father said. "If you don't have the brain to manage it, it's not going to do you any good."

Besides, Shaquille was enjoying college life. In Baton Rouge, he had become a celebrity. Of course, being 7-foot-1 and 295 pounds, he was recognized everywhere he went. One couple, Ernest and Rebecca Long, of nearby Geismar, Louisiana, enjoyed watching Shaquille play so much that they named their son Shaquille O'Neal Long. When Shaquille heard about the baby, he drove to the couple's house and had his picture taken with him. When the O'Neal family came to Baton Rouge for a visit, Shaquille insisted they have dinner with the Long family and baby Shaquille.

Shaquille, a business major, also was popular with LSU's teachers. "I've had a lot of other athletes in classes," said Robert Justis, a professor at the LSU School of Business. "But he reached out more than any athlete I've ever had.

"Shaquille was different, even though it was obvious he was going to make millions as a basketball player," he said. "He sat in the front row and asked good questions. You could tell he wanted to know what to do with all that money. He fit in. And the one thing I really admired was that he respected everyone else. He certainly made me a fan."

Shaquille was growing up fast, but he still had his playful side. He often imitated coach Brown, making teammates laugh when the coach wasn't watching. On road trips, he sometimes woke up teammates with late-night prank calls. Once, he set off fireworks outside the school dormitory.

On the bench, Shaquille has a playful side.

During the summer, he continued to work for Richard Gill, who owns a construction company in Baton Rouge. Once, Gill asked Shaquille and a teammate to do some yard and house work at his home during the Christmas break. Shaquille climbed a ladder to work on the roof, but was momentarily stranded when his teammate moved the ladder. How did Shaquille solve the problem? By jumping off the roof, foolishly risking an injury. He wasn't hurt, but he scared his boss, Gill, half to death.

But Gill mostly remembers Shaquille as one of his hardest workers and a loyal employee. In truth, Shaquille probably could have taken it easy during the summers and Christmas holidays because he would soon be earning millions. But with two younger sisters and a younger brother getting ready for college, Shaquille knew he could help his parents if he paid his own college expenses.

"There were just things that made him so different from most of the guys," Gill said of his 7-foot-1 employee. "He was on time, dependable, and, in a lot of ways, very mature. He was raised well."

The problem was that by his junior season at LSU, it was obvious Shaquille wasn't having as much fun on the basketball court as he would have liked.

Other teams often had three or four players covering Shaquille whenever he had the ball.

More than ever, opposing teams were using zone defenses to surround O'Neal with three and some-times four players each time he caught the ball near the basket. This meant Shaquille had almost no room to take advantage of his size and athletic ability. Each time he got past one defender, he would usually find two or three more in his way.

Shaquille, his father, and coach Brown believed teams played far too rough against him, and they thought the referees weren't doing much about it.

During a Southeastern Conference tournament game against Tennessee in March 1992, Shaquille no longer could contain his frustration. Tennessee's Carlus Groves grabbed Shaquille from behind by the waist while Shaquille was attempting a dunk. Shaquille turned and swung his arm at Groves. Both benches emptied as angry players surged onto the floor, and it was several minutes before the referees could clear the court of players and coaches.

The Southeastern Conference administrators decided to suspend Shaquille from LSU's next conference tournament game. An angry coach Brown said he wouldn't blame Shaquille for leaving after his junior season and jumping to the NBA, where zone defenses are not allowed and players have more freedom to showcase their individual talents.

Coach Brown and Shaquille talk things over during an LSU game.

Shaquille disagrees with a referee's call.

On March 21, 1992, in the second round of the NCAA Tournament, LSU was eliminated by Indiana, 89-79. Shaquille had scored 36 points, pulled down 12 rebounds, and blocked 5 shots. For the season, he had averaged 24.1 points, 14 rebounds, and 5.2 blocked shots for the 21-10 Tigers. But after the Indiana loss, everyone figured Shaquille had played his last college game.

On April 3, he made it official. At a press conference at Fort Sam Houston in San Antonio, near the Cole campus, where he had starred in high school, Shaquille announced he would enter the June NBA draft.

Many young fans share Shaquille's sense of humor.

"I'll miss the students, the fans, the players," Shaquille said of LSU. "I think the experience was very much needed. I'm still a strong believer in a college education. I know you all are probably sitting out there saying, 'That's what they all say.' But I'd like to consider myself as not like the others who have said this. I will continue my education.

"But this year I said to myself, 'Are you having fun?' This past season I wasn't having that much fun," Shaquille said. "I was taught at a young age: If it's not fun, stop playing."

His entire family attended the press conference. And though his parents always wanted him to get a college degree, they supported his decision.

"He's more mature," Harrison said. "He's grown up a lot living by himself and taking care of himself. I don't have any problem with him going to the next level and adapting to the situation. He can be as good as he wants to be as long as he keeps his head together. He doesn't have a big head; he doesn't have an ego."

His mother realized the announcement was an important moment in her son's life. "I'm not sad. I'm happy for him," Lucille Harrison said. "I think anytime you think of the unknown, it kind of scares you a little bit. But he's worked hard and he deserves to do well."

Near the end of the press conference, Shaquille was reminded that only three years before in the nearby Cole gym, he had announced he would attend LSU. Those three years had flown by, Shaquille agreed, but they had been special, too.

"It's gone pretty fast. I've grown a mustache. I'm very handsome now," Shaquille said, drawing a laugh from the dozens of assembled reporters.

The Orlando Magic chose Shaquille with the first pick in the 1992 National Basketball Association draft.

An NBA Force

On May 17, 1992, Orlando Magic general manager Pat Williams sat with representatives from 10 other NBA teams, hoping for the greatest gift a basketball franchise could receive. The occasion was the NBA lottery in Secaucus, New Jersey. Eleven teams were drawing to decide the order in which they would select players in the June 24 draft. One very lucky team would win the right to draft first and select Shaquille O'Neal.

Williams was sitting next to Dallas Mavericks owner Donald Carter. Carter, wearing a huge cowboy hat, was rubbing a small stone for good luck. Carter let Williams rub the stone, too. That might have been a mistake, because a few minutes later, Williams was the one who got lucky. Orlando won the first pick and the opportunity to select Shaquille. Williams' jaw fell open. He leaned back in his chair, amazed and overjoyed.

Back in Florida, the city of Orlando celebrated. That night the Magic opened its ticket window and sold 50 season tickets. By midweek 100 more season tickets had been sold. Everyone was talking about Shaquille O'Neal—The Shaq. Suddenly Orlando, a team that had only existed for three years and had a 70-176 record, had a player around which to build its future.

Just as suddenly, money and national attention began pouring in for Shaquille. Even before he agreed to his $40 million Orlando contract, he signed a $20 million deal just to endorse and wear Reebok's "Shaq Attaq" shoes.

Not even a superstar gets everything he wants.

Shaquille raps with Fu Schnickens on *The Arsenio Hall Show.* Later he released two rap albums. The first, *Shaq Diesel,* went platinum.

Before his rookie season was half over, Shaquille had appeared in a Reebok commercial with legendry NBA centers Wilt Chamberlain, Bill Russell, Kareem Abdul-Jabbar, and Bill Walton. And he had starred in a popular commercial in which he pulls down a basket, asks a small child for a Pepsi, and is told, "Don't even think about it."

Shaquille has been active in the movie world as well. He starred in *Kazaam,* where he played a rapping genie. He even has an autobiography, *Shaq Attaq! My Rookie Year,* lining bookstore shelves.

Shaquille has come a long way from the days when he was a troublemaking adolescent in West Germany, or even a 17-year-old winning a Texas high school championship. But he is still the lovable giant with the crooked smile. And, above all, he still remembers and lives by the values his parents taught him.

As a rookie, Shaquille held his own against NBA star David Robinson of the San Antonio Spurs.

Hakeem Olajuwon couldn't push Shaquille around.

"Money doesn't make people change," Shaquille said. "People make people change and I'm not going to let that happen. The only difference money makes is material things. It just means a couple more cars, leather jackets."

On the court, there seems to be no limit to how good Shaquille can be. During his rookie season, Orlando was 41-41, a dramatic turnaround from its 21-61 finish the season before.

"When you are 7 feet tall, you're supposed to have limitations," Lakers center Sam Bowie said of Shaquille. "But I haven't seen any."

In time Shaquille will learn fundamentals that will make him a better NBA player—little things like better footwork around the basket, working on his turnaround shot, or even perfecting the hook shot. So far, his sheer size and strength alone have made him hard to stop. If anyone had doubts about Shaquille's ability during his rookie season, they surely were convinced on February 7, 1993. That afternoon, three minutes into a nationally televised game between Orlando and Phoenix, Shaquille literally brought down a backboard. He drove the lane for a dunk, hung on the rim, and the combination of his strength and 305-pound body snapped a steel hook in the post that held the backboard. The game was delayed 37 minutes while a new backboard was installed.

Not since 7-foot Wilt Chamberlain entered the NBA in 1959 has a player made an impact on the league the way Shaquille has. He was selected NBA Player of the Week in his first week as a rookie, something that had never happened before. He also was named NBA Player of the Month in his first month, another first.

Fans appreciate Shaquille, not just for his ability but for the fun he has on the court. The year before Shaquille arrived, Orlando was 24th out of 27 teams in the number of fans who attended its road games. During his rookie season, Orlando was second in NBA road attendance, behind only Michael Jordan's Chicago Bulls.

"The league needs someone like Shaquille O'Neal," said Jordan. "He's going to be a great player."

Shaquille continued to dazzle fans in the 1993–1994 season. His powerful playing, including a league-leading 387 dunks, helped the Magic's record improve to 50–32. The team, for the first time ever, advanced to the play-offs, where it lost to Indiana in the first round.

The following season, Orlando once again made the play-offs. The Magic beat Boston, Chicago, and Indiana to make it to the NBA Finals against the Houston Rockets. Shaquille averaged 28 points per game, but the Rockets defeated the Magic in four games.

Shaquille, however, is determined to one day win a championship. "The main thing is he wants to be a better basketball player," said Orlando guard Dennis Scott, one of Shaquille's best friends on the team. "He wants to get a championship ring."

"Coming into the league, I didn't know what to think," Shaquille told a group of reporters before a game in Dallas. "But it's really not hard. Sign autographs. Come talk to you guys for 20 minutes before the game and 20 minutes after the game. It's going from city to city, playing against All-Stars—guys you saw on TV when you were growing up. I'm out there showcasing my talents— dunking, diving on the floor, having fun. That's what it's all about."

The hardest adjustment Shaquille has had to make is off the court. Autograph seekers surround him almost everywhere he goes. When Orlando plays in other cities, Shaquille often checks in at hotels with a fake name so fans can't phone his room.

"I can't go to the mall, I can't go to a big restaurant," he said. "Unless I absolutely have to, I don't go out in public."

When he wants time to himself, he drives around in his Ford Explorer. It gives him a chance to think. When he does go out to eat, he likes to keep it simple. He likes to go to smaller restaurants, where people get personal service.

Before most home games, Shaquille goes to Pisa Italian Pizza, a small restaurant in a shopping center. The owner, whom Shaquille calls "Mamma," brings him the same meal before every game: spaghetti and meatballs, two slices of cheese pizza, and a large orange soda.

Although being famous keeps Shaquille from going out as often as he would like, it has not changed his relationship with his family. His parents remained in San Antonio through most of Shaquille's first NBA season. But when Philip Harrison retired from the military that summer, Shaquille moved his parents, sisters Lateefah and Ayesha, and brother Jamal to Orlando.

Philip Harrison carefully watches Shaquille's career.

A moment Philip Harrison will never forget oc-
curred during the NBA All-Star weekend in Salt
Lake City, Utah, midway through Shaquille's
rookie season. When the NBA presented each player with an All-Star game ring, Shaquille looked at
his ring for a few minutes, then gave it to his

father. A proud Harrison wore the ring for the rest of the weekend.

As jam-packed as this young superstar's life has been, 1996 was a whirlwind of success and change. Shaquille won the NBA scoring title, averaging 26.6 points in the 1995–96 season. He also led Orlando to the 1996 NBA Eastern Conference finals, only to suffer a defeat by Chicago.

Shaquille was disappointed because he had long wanted to win that prestigious NBA champion-ship title. Coaches and fans said that this was a major reason he decided to switch teams before the 1996–97 season. Before the playoffs, one coach predicted, "The decision [to switch teams] may well hinge on whether he wins the title." And switch teams Shaquille did.

On July 1, 1996, he became a free agent, en-abling him to choose which team he wanted to join. "My final decision was to play for the Los Angeles Lakers. I felt that a change was neces-sary," Shaquille said. "Change is for the good and change is for the better. This was a dream."

That year he fulfilled another dream. He was a proud member of the 1996 gold medal-winning U.S. Olympic basketball team, the Dream Team. Shaq, along with other basketball superstars like Grant Hill and Scottie Pippen, defeated Yugoslavia 95–69 in the gold medal game.

One thing Shaquille will never have to worry about is money. His seven-year contract of approximately $120 million with the Lakers will pay him an average of $17.4 million per season.

Money hasn't spoiled him, however. He sticks to what his parents taught him. Those who have met Shaquille find him to be well mannered, easygoing, and respectful to others. And he is still committed to his education. He uses the offseasons to continue working toward his degree at Louisiana State University.

His action-packed life, filled with important decisions and responsibilities, hasn't changed his fun-loving spirit, however. "Really, I am more mature," said Shaq, "but I'm still a kid now and then."

SHAQUILLE O'NEAL'S
BASKETBALL STATISTICS

Louisiana State University

Year	Games	FGM-FGA	%	FTM-FTA	%	Rbds	RPG	Pts	PPG
89–90	32	180–314	.573	85–153	.556	385	12.0	445	13.9
90–91	28	312–497	.628	150–235	.638	411	14.7	774	27.6
91–92	30	294–478	.615	134–254	.528	421	14	722	24.1
Totals	90	786–1289	.610	369–642	.575	1217	13.5	1941	21.6

College highlights:

—Named to *The Sporting News* All-America first team in 1990 and 1991
—Led NCAA Division I basketball players with 14.7 rebounds a game in 1991
—Led NCAA Division I basketball players with 5.2 blocked shots a game in 1992

Orlando Magic, Regular Season

Year	Games	FGM-FGA	%	FTM-FTA	%	Rbds	RPG	Pts	PPG	Blks
92–93	81	733–1304	.562	427–721	.592	1122	13.9	1893	23.4	286
93–94	81	953–1591	.599	471–850	.554	1072	13.2	2377	29.3	231
94–95	79	930–1594	.583	455–854	.533	901	11.4	2315	29.3	192
95–96	54	592–1033	.573	249–511	.487	596	11.0	1434	26.6	115

Orlando Magic, Play-offs

Year	Games	FGM-FGA	%	FTM-FTA	%	Rbds	RPG	Pts	PPG	Blks
93–94	3	23–45	.511	16–34	.471	40	13.3	62	20.7	9
94–95	21	195–338	.577	149–261	.571	250	11.9	539	25.7	40
95–96	12	131–216	.606	48–122	.393	120	10.0	310	25.8	15

National Basketball Association highlights

—Selected with the first pick in the NBA draft in 1992
—Chosen NBA Rookie of the Year in 1993
—Named to NBA All-Rookie first team in 1993
—Chosen for the NBA All-Star game in 1993, 1994
—Named to the All-NBA third team in 1994
—Named to the All-NBA second team in 1995
—Named to the All-NBA third team in 1996

ACKNOWLEDGMENTS

Photographs are reproduced with the permission of: p. 1, Reuters/Bettmann; pp. 2, 53, 56, AP/Wide World Photos; pp. 6, 11, 54, 55, Barry Gossage; pp. 9 (both), 38, 40, 43, 45, 46, 47, 48, 59, Brad Messina; pp. 15, 22, 25, 30, 34, 37, 39, Andy King; pp. 17, 18, Walter A. Collis, Jr.; p. 27, Cole High School; pp. 29, 33, Lynne Dobson/Austin American Statesman; p. 50, Brian Drake/SportsChrome East/West; p. 52, Courtesy of Pepsico, Inc.; p. 58, Jon Hayt; p. 61, Nathaniel Butler/*Sports Illustrated;* p. 63, John Biever.

Front cover photograph by Brad Mangin/Duomo. Back cover photograph by John Kuntz/Archive Photos.